CELEBRATING
LENT

D0191375

REV. JUDE WINKLER, OFM Conv.

Imprimi Potest: Mark Curesky, OFM Conv., Minister Provincial of St. Anthony of Padua Province (USA)
Nihil Obstat: Francis J. McAree, S.T.D., Censor Librorum
Imprimatur: ✠ **Patrick J. Sheridan, D.D.**, Vicar General, Archdiocese of New York

Printed in Hong Kong

GOD'S LOVE FOR US

THE greatest sign of God's love for us is the fact that He sent His only Son into this world. He died in order to save us from our sins.

Jesus taught about this love when He traveled around His homeland for three years. He called upon His people to turn from their selfish ways. He performed many miracles, healing those who were blind, lame, or suffering in any way. Many people did not want to turn from their sins. They arrested Jesus and had Him put to death. They nailed Him to a Cross.

Jesus did not resist. Even though He could have called Angels from the heavens to rescue Him, He did not. Rather, He accepted His sufferings as peacefully as a lamb. He realized that He was dying for us, to set us free from our sins.

So on Good Friday Jesus died on the Cross and was buried, but God did not allow Jesus to be defeated. On Easter Sunday, God raised Jesus from the dead. Jesus appeared to His disciples and promised that He would never leave them alone. He and the Father would send the Spirit to guide the Church until the end of time.

3

PREPARING FOR EASTER

FROM its earliest days, the Church has celebrated these saving mysteries. Easter was probably the very first holy day that Christians agreed should be celebrated every year.

Easter was so holy a feast that people very soon realized that they should spend some time preparing for it. At first they would fast and pray for only a day or two.

Even in these early days some people spent more time preparing for Easter. They were the men and women who were to be baptized on Easter Sunday. They had been preparing to enter the Church for a long time, but now they would begin several weeks of special prayer and fasting.

Yet, at first, no one was sure how long that time of prayer should be. Then they realized that Jesus had given them an example. He had first gone down to the Jordan River where He was baptized by John the Baptist. The heavens had opened and God had proclaimed that Jesus was His only Son. Then He went out into the desert in order to prepare for His mission to preach the Word of God. He fasted and prayed for forty days and forty nights in order to be ready to do God's will.

FORTY DAYS OF LENT

WHILE Jesus was in the desert, the devil tempted Him. Jesus was hungry after forty days of fasting, so the devil told Him to turn stones into bread. Jesus refused, for He would not use His power for His own comfort.

The devil then offered Jesus all the kingdoms of the world if only He would worship him. Jesus refused, for He worshiped only the Father.

Finally, the devil asked Jesus to throw Himself down from the walls of the temple to show that the Angels would protect Him. Jesus would not do this, for He would not put God to the test.

Jesus then left the desert and began to call people to follow God's way. The forty days in the desert had been a time for Jesus to reject the devil's call and once again to choose God's call.

Forty days also reminded people of the forty years that the people of Israel had spent in the desert after they had left their slavery in Egypt. This, too, was a time of preparation, as the people of Israel purified their hearts before they entered the Promised Land.

8

PREPARING FOR BAPTISM

THUS, when the people about to be baptized in the early Church wanted to know how long they should prepare, they decided upon forty days. Like Jesus, they were preparing to listen to the Father's call with their whole hearts.

Like the people of Israel who had left slavery and learned to trust in God's love, they were leaving slavery to sin and entering the Church, God's Promised Land. And so those who were preparing for Baptism fasted and prayed for forty days and forty nights before the great feast of Easter.

They, in turn, became examples for the whole Church. Soon even men and women who had long since been baptized decided to join them in fasting and praying. They realized that this would be a good chance for them to look at their lives and ask themselves how faithful they had been in keeping their baptismal promises.

Then, at the Easter Vigil, as some in the community were being baptized, the others would renew their baptismal promises. They all celebrated their death to their old way of life and their birth to a new life in the risen Jesus.

THE RITE OF CHRISTIAN INITIATION

LENT and Easter are still times to prepare for Baptism and to turn from sin.

In recent years, the Church has developed a program for adults preparing for their Baptism. It is called the Rite of Christian Initiation. When babies are baptized, they are baptized any time of the year. But when people who are older are to be baptized, they go through a long time of preparation. They study about the faith for many months. Then, during Lent, they enter a special period of prayer and fasting, just as the early Christians had done.

For the rest of us, Lent is a time when we remember the promises we made long ago at our Baptism. On Easter Sunday, we light candles and we are blessed with holy water as we are asked to make our baptismal promises once again.

Lent is also a special time for one of the other Sacraments. Because Lent is a time to turn from sin, it is a very good time to celebrate the Sacrament of Reconciliation. Most parishes have special penance services so that we can celebrate God's forgiveness as a community.

12

ASH WEDNESDAY

TODAY we call the forty days during which we prepare for Easter "Lent." This name comes from an Old English word that means the "Spring," for Lent begins toward the end of Winter and leads us into the season of Spring.

The actual date for the beginning of Lent depends upon the date of Easter. Unlike Christmas Day, which is the same date every year, Easter moves from year to year. It falls on the Sunday after the first full moon after the beginning of Spring. Thus, it can fall any time between the end of March and the end of April.

Lent begins six and one half weeks before that date. It can begin between mid-February and mid-March. We begin Lent on Ash Wednesday. On that day we go to church to receive ashes on our heads. These ashes are a sign that we are entering a time of penance.

When the priest places the ashes on our head, he says either, "Remember, man, that you are dust, and unto dust you shall return," or "Repent and believe in the Gospel." Both of these sayings remind us of how precious time is and how we should use it to grow closer to God.

SIGNS OF LENT

BEGINNING with Ash Wednesday, there are a number of reminders for us that we are in a holy season.

All throughout the year, priests wear different colored vestments. They might wear white or green or red vestments, depending upon the feast that we are celebrating. During Lent, priests almost always wear purple as a reminder that we are in a time of penance.

We celebrate hardly any other feasts during Lent because it is such an important time of the year. Parishes have as few celebrations as possible. There are no dances or parties or weddings throughout Lent, for it is a time to be more serious.

During the Mass, we also have reminders that the season is more serious. We do not sing the Alleluia before the Gospel or in any of the other songs. Alleluia is a word that reminds us of Easter; so during Lent we do not say it at all.

We do not sing or say the "Glory to God in the highest" during Mass. We have fewer songs and fewer flowers, for everything should be very simple during Lent.

15

HOLY SCRIPTURE

THERE is one part of the liturgy that is more important during Lent. It is the part containing the Scripture readings that we use at Mass for the weekdays and for Sundays. They are all specially selected to tell the story of our Redemption.

The Old Testament readings tell us the story of how people were created by God but then turned to sin. In the days of Noah, God purified the earth by sending a great flood.

God then chose a people through Abraham. He guided and protected them even in the days of Joseph when there was a great famine. He saved His people from slavery in Egypt. He led them under Moses to the Promised Land.

God sent Prophets to guide His people, but the people and the kings of Israel would not listen to them. During Lent, we hear the loving words of men like Isaiah, Jeremiah, and Ezekiel.

The New Testament readings are also important, for we hear of how Jesus called His followers to be converted from their sins. An important part of our participation in Lent is to listen to these readings with great attention.

FASTING

ANOTHER part of our Lenten preparation is fasting. From its earliest days, Lent was a time to give up certain things that people enjoy throughout the year. Long ago, the fasting was very serious. People would eat only one meal a day. From Ash Wednesday on they would eat no fish or meat. They would have no eggs or cheese or milk. In some places, people would fast like this for five days a week, while in others they would fast every day except for Sunday.

Today we do not fast in the same way as they once did. One of the things that we do is to eat no meat on any Friday during Lent. We can eat fish or cheese or any other thing as long as it has no meat.

On Ash Wednesday and Good Friday we also have special rules. Those who are over 21 years old and less than 59 years old and in good health are obliged to fast. They may eat one full meal and have two other smaller ones that together do not equal one full meal.

The reason that we fast is to remind us that God is more important than food. We also fast to share the pain of those who do not have enough to eat.

GOOD DEEDS

ONE of the other reasons that we fast during Lent is that it gives us a chance to share our food with those who are hungry. We put aside the money we would have spent on food or candy and we give it to those who do not have enough to eat. We respond to Jesus' call to feed the hungry, visit the sick, and comfort those who are sad.

During Lent, we try to be more generous with our time and our love. We ask whether any things we have been doing are selfish, and we promise to change those things.

It is especially important to begin with our own family and friends. We should help our parents more around the house. We should not fight with our brothers or sisters. We should visit our grandparents or send them a letter. We should pay attention in school and not cause problems.

While we do all of this, we should not forget those who are farther away. We could collect food and blankets for a soup kitchen in our city. We could also pray for people we see suffering on the TV news.

A TIME OF PRAYER

WE have talked about how we prepare for Easter by our Lenten readings at Mass, our fasting, and our acts of charity. There is one other thing that has been part of Lenten preparations from the earliest times. It is prayer.

There are four reasons why we pray. In prayer we *adore God*, praising God for His greatness.

In prayer we *ask for things that we need.* We depend on God for everything, and our prayer can remind us of that.

In prayer we *give thanks to God* for all the good things that He has given us. And finally, in prayer *we ask for forgiveness* of all our sins.

All four of these types of prayer are important during Lent. We see the greatness of God in the fact that Jesus died for us; so we should praise God. As we fast, we remember that all of our food, and even everything we have, is really a gift from God. We should ask God for everything that we need and thank Him for everything that we have. Finally, as we have already seen, Lent is a time to turn from our sins; so we can use prayer to tell God that we are sorry.

23

THE WAY OF THE CROSS

ANOTHER form of prayer that we use during Lent is to meditate on what Jesus did for us in His Passion and Death. It is important for us to hear the story of Jesus' sufferings so that we can know how much He loves us.

One of the ways that we hear this story is by praying the Way of the Cross. In this prayer we remember fourteen different things that happened to Jesus on Good Friday. (These are called Stations.) We hear of how He was condemned to death, took His Cross, and fell under its weight three times. We hear of Him meeting His Mother, the women of Jerusalem, the kindly Veronica who wiped His face, and Simon who helped Him carry the Cross.

In the last Stations we hear of how He was nailed to the Cross and how He died. His body was then taken down from the Cross and buried. All of this tells us how much Jesus loved us.

During Lent we will also have the chance to think about the Cross of Jesus and to kiss it on Good Friday. It reminds us that every time we make the Sign of the Cross, we are remembering how Jesus died for us.

PALM SUNDAY

HOLY Week is the climax of our preparations for Easter. It begins on Palm Sunday when we mark Jesus' entry into Jerusalem.

The celebration on Palm Sunday begins with a presentation of what happened that first Palm Sunday. We gather outside of the church or at the front door of the church. We hear the Gospel story of how Jesus rode on a donkey and entered the city of Jerusalem.

As Jesus rode along, the people gathered up branches from the trees and waved them in the air. They took their clothes and laid them down before the donkey. They cried, "Hosanna to the son of David," proclaiming Jesus as their king.

Next, we take our own palms, which are then blessed. (In some countries olive branches are used instead of palms.) We process with those branches into our church.

There is another powerful reminder of Holy Week during the Palm Sunday Mass. At the Gospel time we hear the entire story of the Passion, Suffering, and Death of Jesus. This is a good introduction to Holy Week. We pray and remember the importance of what Christ did for us and how we should respond to His love.

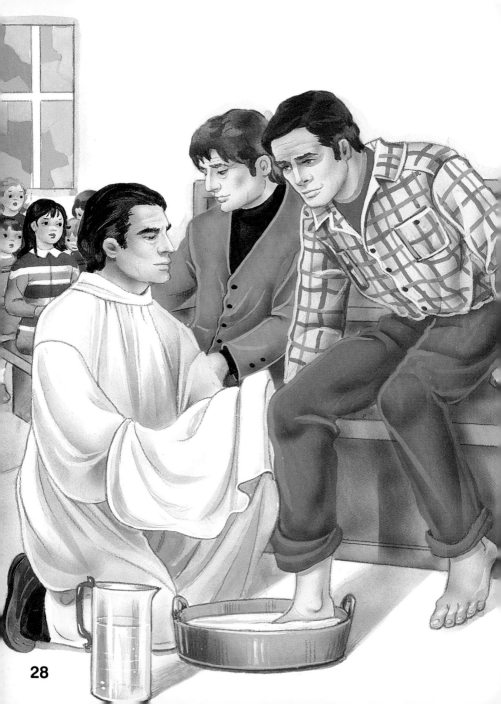

28

HOLY THURSDAY

THE next important event is Holy Thursday. On Holy Thursday morning the bishop gathers with people from all over his diocese for a special Mass in the Cathedral. At that Mass he blesses the oils that will be used all throughout the diocese for the rest of the year. These oils will be used in the Sacraments of Baptism, Confirmation, Holy Orders, and Anointing of the Sick.

Later that evening each parish gathers to celebrate the Lord's Last Supper. At that Mass we hear the Gospel of how Jesus washed the feet of His disciples. He was teaching them that He was giving His life for them, and they should be willing to give their lives for each other.

After the homily, we then relive that first Last Supper, for the priest puts on an apron and like Jesus washes the feet of a number of people from the community.

At the end of the Mass, we take the Eucharist and process with it to another part of the church. We clear off the altar and leave the church empty. This reminds us that we are entering a time to remember the Death of Jesus, a time of great sorrow and pain.

GOOD FRIDAY

ON Good Friday, we relive the Passion of our Lord. This is not really a Mass, for we do not celebrate any Masses between Holy Thursday night and the Vigil Mass on Holy Saturday night. The priest enters in silence and lies down to pray before the altar. After a few minutes, he rises and we have an opening prayer.

Next, we hear readings from the Old Testament and the New Testament, but the most important reading is the account of the Passion from the Gospel of John. When we hear of how Jesus died on the Cross, we all fall on our knees for a few minutes of silence.

Afterward, we pray for those who are Catholics, for all Christians, for the Jewish people, for people who believe in God, for our leaders, and for everyone who needs our prayers.

Then we honor the Cross. We process up to the altar to kiss the Cross as a sign of our gratitude for what Jesus has done.

In the last part of our ceremony we receive Communion from the Hosts that were consecrated the night before.

HOLY SATURDAY

AFTER receiving Communion on Good Friday, we say a final prayer and go home. Our long preparations of fasting and praying, of doing good deeds and listening to the story of Jesus' Life and Death has come to an end. It is now time to wait.

All throughout Holy Saturday we wait for evening to arrive so that we can bless our Paschal fire and holy water.

That Saturday evening we gather once again. We hear the Gospel that proclaims that Jesus is risen. We hear the great hymn, "Glory to God in the Highest," sung once again, and we all sing the great Alleluia.